MY ZONE

MY ZONE

MY MOVIE SLEEPOVER

ANITA GANERI

EDGE
FRANKLIN WATTS
LONDON•SYDNEY

**FIRST PUBLISHED IN 2010 BY
FRANKLIN WATTS
338 EUSTON ROAD
LONDON NW1 3BH**

FRANKLIN WATTS AUSTRALIA
LEVEL 17/207 KENT STREET
SYDNEY NSW 2000

COPYRIGHT © FRANKLIN WATTS 2010

SERIES EDITOR: ADRIAN COLE
ART DIRECTOR: JONATHAN HAIR
DESIGN: BLUE PAW DESIGN
PICTURE RESEARCH: DIANA MORRIS
CONSULTANT: FIONA M. COLLINS,
    ROEHAMPTON UNIVERSITY

ISBN: 978 0 7496 9569 9

DEWEY CLASSIFICATION: 793. 2

ACKNOWLEDGEMENTS:
Action Press/Rex Features: 25t. ADC/Rex Features: 36. Bandido
Images/Shutterstock: 35. Alex Berliner/BEI/Rex Features: 16t,
40. Bikeriderlondon/Shutterstock: 13. Fernando Blanco Calzada/
Shutterstock: 21c. Blaneyphoto/istockphoto: 27b. Evgenia
Bolyukh/Shutterstock: 21br. Peter Brooker/Rex Features: 29t. Sean
De Burca/Shutterstock: 41bl. Humberto Carreno/Rex Features:
23b. Carroteater/Shutterstock: 21bl. Coprid/Shutterastock:
20c. Adrian Denis/Rex Features: 11t. © Walt Disney/Everett/
Rex Features: 42t, 42b. © Walt Disney/Kobal/Picture Desk: 16b.
Mary Evans PL: 8. Everett Collection/Rex Features: 22, 32, 33,
FimkaJane/Shutterstock: 34br. Maxim Godkin/Shutterstock:
21t. Gravicam/Shutterstock: 41br. Ken Inness/Shutterstock: 39t.
Juice Images/Alamy: 7. Jeff Kravitz/Getty Images: 11b. Alexey
Khromushin/Shutterstock: 39b. Rick Legg/istockphoto: 14. Mates/
Shutterstock: 38. MCP/Rex Features: 28. Ryan McVay/Getty
Images: 43t. Miramax/Everett Collection/Rex Features: 17b.
Monkey Business Images/Shutterstock: 27t. Most Wanted/Rex
Features: 29b. Newspix/Rex Features: 18. Nikada/istockphoto:
4, 5. Trinette Reed/Shutetrstock: 31t. Rex Features: 19b, 23t, 25b.
Simon Roberts/Rex Features: 37b. Chris Rout/Alamy: 26. Igor
Shikov/Shutterstock: 20t. Sipa Press/Rex Features: 41c. SNAP/
Rex Features: 10. Kallash K Soni/Shutterstock: 12. Igor Stepovik/
Shutterstock: 31b. StockLife/Shutterstock: 41t. Charlie Stone/
Alamy: 37t. Supri Suharjoto/Shutterstock: 34l. Unimedia Images/
Rex Features: 43b. Universal/Playtone/Kobal Collection/Picture
Desk: 19. Universal/SNAP/Rex Features: 17t. Warner Brothers/
Everett Collection/Rex Features: 6. Warner Brothers/Kobal
Collection/Picture Desk: 9. Elliot Westacott/Shutterstock: 21bc.
Weststudio24h/Stutterstock: 15. Iyonne Wierink/Shutterstock:
20bl. Debby Wong/Shutterstock: 24. Anton Zabielskyi/
Shutterstock: 30.

EVERY ATTEMPT HAS BEEN MADE TO CLEAR COPYRIGHT.
SHOULD THEIR BE ANY INADVERTENT OMISSION PLEASE
APPLY TO THE PUBLISHER FOR RETIFICATION

PRINTED IN CHINA

FRANKLIN WATTS IS A DIVISION OF
HACHETTE CHILDREN'S BOOKS,
AN HACHETTE UK COMPANY.
WWW.HACHETTE.CO.UK

Please note: every effort has been made by the Publishers to
ensure that the websites in this book contain no inappropriate
or offensive material. However, because of the nature of the
Internet, it is impossible to guarantee that the contents of
these sites will not be altered. We strongly advise that Internet
access is supervised by a responsible adult.

LOOK OUT FOR...

Words highlighted in the text can be found in the glossary.

"Hi, we're rolling out the red carpet for **MY ZONE** *My Movie Sleepover. It's packed with movie stars, film buff stuff and sensational sleepover tips. I can't wait! "*

Anita x

IT'S MY MOVIE SLEEPOVER

Can you imagine a world without movies? It is almost impossible. From the glamour of Hollywood to the bling of Bollywood, movies and movie stars are everywhere – on the TV, online or at the cinema.

WEBtag

You will see WEBtags throughout this book. Many of the websites feature more information about the articles, videos and up-to-date news and blogs.

If you're mad about the movies, why not invite your friends round for a massive movie sleepover? Dress up as movie stars, pop in a DVD, grab some popcorn and it's lights, camera, action all the way (until your mum and dad tell you it's time to sleep, of course!)

 There's more to a movie sleepover than bouncing around on your bed!

Inside this book, you'll find loads of ideas to help you plan the perfect sleepover – from designing your invites to picking a movie. Plus there are lots of facts from the movie world to chat about.

MOVIE MILESTONES

The movie industry makes, sells and shows movies around the world. Today it's worth billions of pounds, but the first movies were nothing like the ones you watch today. Check out these movie milestones...

1893 American Thomas Edison invented the Kinetoscope to show moving black-and-white pictures. Only one person at a time could view the movie through a small eyepiece.

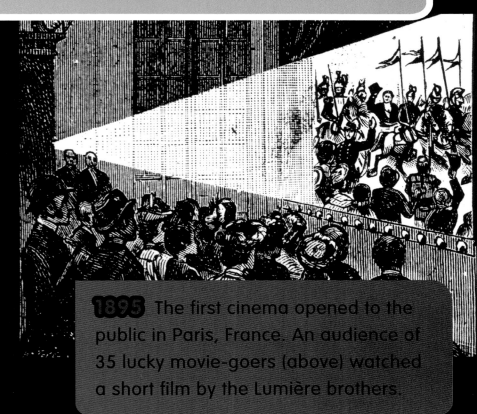

1895 The first cinema opened to the public in Paris, France. An audience of 35 lucky movie-goers (above) watched a short film by the Lumière brothers.

WEBtag Find out more about the people behind some early movie milestones, including the Lumière brothers.

www.earlycinema.com

1927 *The Jazz Singer* was the first feature-length '**talkie**' with a soundtrack. Before this, lines of speech appeared on the screen for viewers to read or a musician played live music.

1929 The first Oscar (Academy Awards®) ceremony was held in Hollywood, USA. The 'Golden Age' of Hollywood movies had begun.

1932 The invention of a film process called Technicolor meant movies could now be filmed in colour, rather than black-and-white.

1950s Cinema screens got bigger and bolder as wide-screen movies became popular. But films now had to be **shot on location** because sets looked really fake.

1975/6 VHS video format made it possible for people to buy or rent films and watch them at home.

1985 The first CG (computer-generated) character appeared in the movie *Young Sherlock Holmes*. By the 1990s, CGI (computer-generated imagery) **blockbusters** like *Jurassic Park* and *Toy Story* (shown) were the talk of the movie world.

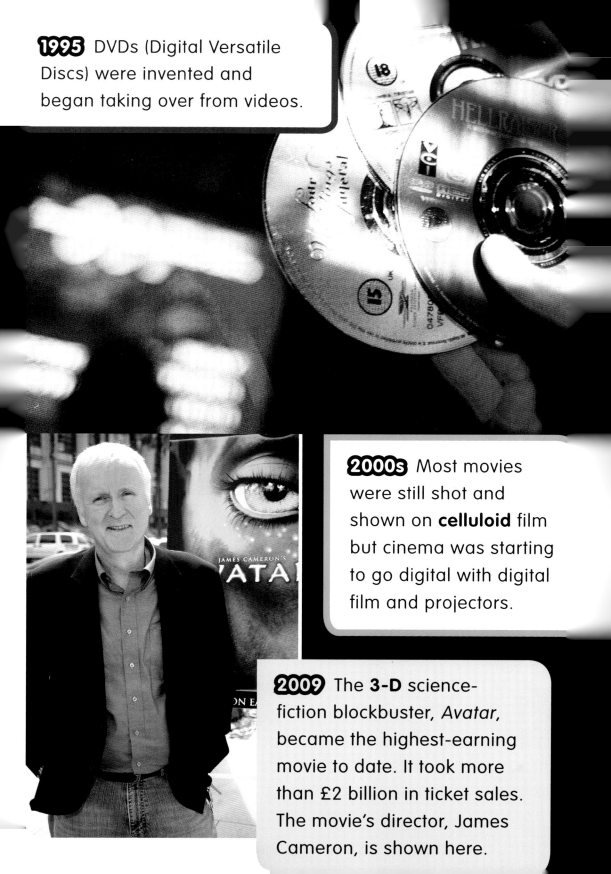

1995 DVDs (Digital Versatile Discs) were invented and began taking over from videos.

2000s Most movies were still shot and shown on **celluloid** film but cinema was starting to go digital with digital film and projectors.

2009 The **3-D** science-fiction blockbuster, *Avatar*, became the highest-earning movie to date. It took more than £2 billion in ticket sales. The movie's director, James Cameron, is shown here.

MY MOVIE SLEEPOVER

Thinking of hosting your own movie sleepover? Want to make it the star-studded event of the year? From designing your own invites to choosing a movie, our step-by-step sleepover guide has got everything you'll need.

1 Pick your party theme...

Go for something with plenty of glitz and glamour, like a Hollywood-themed party. That will give you loads of ideas for food, decorations, games and costumes, and it'll make your guests feel like movie stars.

Swop the boas for silk saris and the headbands for bangles, and make it a Bollywood party instead. Grab a DVD of an all-action Bollywood movie and sample some tasty Indian sweets (below).

WEBtag Webpage outlining one way to hold a sleepover.

http://www.coolest-kid-birthday-parties.com/
teenage-slumber-party.html

2 Send out your invites...

Make your own Hollywood-themed invites in the style of movie tickets or Walk of Fame stars (see page 29). Use the sort of wording you'd find on a movie poster.

You are invited to the movie event of the year!

MY HOLLYWOOD MOVIE SLEEPOVER

Starring ...[your name]
Showing at: [date; time; place]
Featuring: movies; games; party food and lots more
Dress: Hollywood glamour

3 Pick your movie...

What sort of movie do you think your friends will like?

- A musical with a cool soundtrack?
- A creepy vampire or ghost story?
- A weepy movie you can sob along to?
- A laugh-a-minute comedy?
- An action-packed adventure?

Give your guests the star treatment by having a red carpet ready to walk on as they come in. Use an old piece of cloth or carpet, or buy a disposable red plastic tablecloth from a party shop.

4 Decorate your bedroom...

Go for a bold colour scheme in ritzy red, black, gold and silver. Add lots of streamers and balloons. Make your own 'wall of fame' by downloading photos of your favourite movie stars and hanging them on the wall in star-shaped frames. Finish off with a '**VIP** Entrance Only' sign on your bedroom door.

5 Give out some goodie bags

Finish your sleepover in style by giving your guests a Hollywood-themed goodie bag. Decorate the bags with glitter and stars, and fill them with sweets, stickers, nail gems, lip gloss and nail varnish.

DID YOU KNOW?

Nominees at the 2010 Oscars received a goodie bag worth £60,000! Each bag was packed with fabulous pressies, including tickets for an African safari, entry to an exclusive fitness resort and a Tiffany crystal-studded cat collar. Phew!

http://www.teenhollywood.com

WEBtag Up-to-date Hollywood movie news.

MOVIE GENRES

Musicals make great sleepover movies, but are you ready to get to grips with some other movie genres? That's the name that movie experts give to the different movie types.

COMEDY

Funny and quirky characters get caught up in hilarious **plots**, providing lots of laughs. Ones to watch: *Ice Age*; *Hotel for Dogs*; *Kung Fu Panda* (right, Jack Black is the voice of Po the panda); *Night at the Museum*.

ADVENTURE

Fast-paced and exciting, and packed with action, spectacular stunts and special effects. Ones to watch: *Indiana Jones*; *Twilight Saga*; *Titanic*; *Karate Kid*; *Pirates of the Caribbean* (left).

WALT DISNEY PICTURES
PRESENTS

PIRATES of the CARIBBEAN

AT WORLD'S END

16

A STEVEN SPIELBERG FILM

E.T.

THE EXTRA-TERRESTRIAL
IN HIS ADVENTURE ON EARTH

FAMILY

Something for everyone, so you can watch it with your mates, or with your gran. Ones to watch: *Babe*; *E.T. (left)*; *Shrek*; *Bend It Like Beckham*; *The Lion King*; *Toy Story*.

SCIENCE FICTION

Often set in a future world, with way-out technology, and weirded-out characters. Ones to watch: *Back to the Future*; *Star Wars*; *Spider Man*.

FANTASY

Stories set in an imaginary world. Ones to watch: *Lord of the Rings*; *Alice in Wonderland*; *Harry Potter*; *The Golden Compass*; *The Princess Bride*.

ROMANTIC COMEDIES

Also known as 'chick flicks', two people fall in love, with a must-have happy ending. Ones to watch: *Bride and Prejudice*; *Ghost*; *Love Actually*; *10 Things I Hate About You*; *Wild Child*.

http://www.filmsite.org/genres.html

WEBtag Lots more examples of different movie genres.

MUST-SEE MOVIES

Can't decide which movie to choose for your sleepover? There are hundreds to pick from. Here are some must-see movies to get your party started.

Zac Efron leaps to the beat in *High School Musical* during one of many catchy songs.

High School Musical

Starring: Zac Efron; Vanessa Hudgens; Ashley Tisdale

Plot: Troy Bolton (Zac Efron) and Gabriella Montez (Vanessa Hudgens) are two teenagers from different backgrounds. They meet at a party and instantly click. Later, at high school, they **audition** for the school musical. But will their jealous friends destroy their friendship?

Mamma Mia

Starring: Meryl Streep, Pierce Brosnan, Amanda Seyfried

Plot: Without telling her mother, 20-year-old bride-to-be, Sophie Sheridan (Amanda Seyfried), invites three men to her wedding on a Greek island. But which one of them is her father? The events are played out to a background of Abba songs.

WEBtag Video clip and trailer for *Mamma Mia* on this movie database.

http://www.imdb.com/title/tt0795421

Camp Rock

Starring: The Jonas Brothers; Demi Lovato

Plot: Mitchie Torres (Demi Lovato) dreams of becoming a singer. At 'Camp Rock', pop star Shane Gray (Joe Jonas) hears singing and falls in love with the voice – but doesn't know it's Mitchie! But how will he feel when he finds out?

SLEEPOVER BAG

Your invite has arrived and the date is in your diary. Now you just need to decide what to pack in your sleepover bag. Here's our guide to the top ten sleepover must-haves...

1 Eyemask: for when you do finally want to get some sleep. Perfect for stopping the morning light waking you up too early!

2 Mobile: for bragging about what a brilliant time you're having to your mates.

3 Pamper bag: make sure it's well stocked with nail varnish, lip gloss, hair brush, make-up and glitter for your party pamper session.

4 Toothbrush: for that dazzling white Hollywood smile.

5 Magazines: for catching up on all the latest movie-star gossip and cool celeb beauty tips.

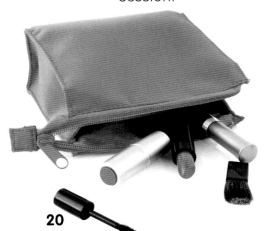

6 Sunglasses: no self-respecting Hollywood star would be seen dead without a pair of these. The bigger, the better.

7 Pjs: splash out on a new pair of pjs or team up an old pair with a fabulous feather boa for a movie-star look.

8 MP3 player: pack your playlist with loads of top tunes to fight off the urge to go to sleep!

9 Sleeping bag: okay so it's not very Hollywood, but you'll regret not taking one if you end up sleeping on the floor.

10 Pumps: the perfect footwear for chilling out in when your movie-star heels stop seeming like a good idea.

MOVIE STAR SECRETS

You've seen their faces in films and glossy magazines, but what are movie stars really like? Prepare to be seriously star-struck as you come face-to-face with some 'A' list celebs.

ROBERT PATTINSON

Ace English actor, Robert (born 1986), appeared as Cedric Diggory in *Harry Potter and the Goblet of Fire* before landing the role of vampire Edward Cullen in the *Twilight Saga*. Tall, dark and handsome, 'RPatz' is now one of the hottest stars around. He also plays the guitar and piano, and writes his own songs. Cool!

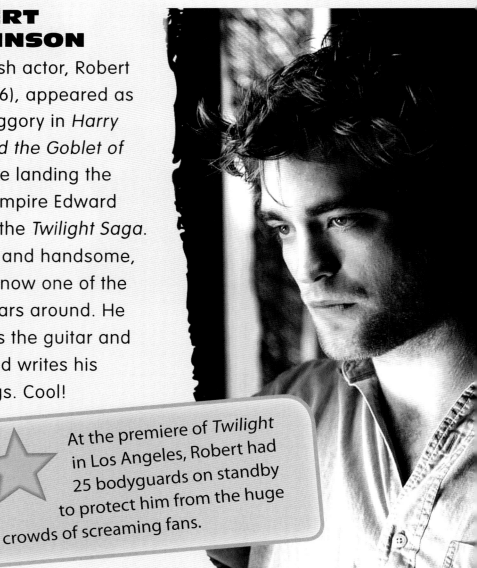

At the premiere of *Twilight* in Los Angeles, Robert had 25 bodyguards on standby to protect him from the huge crowds of screaming fans.

MEGAN FOX

Gorgeous Megan (born 1986) began dancing and acting at the age of five. Today, thanks to her role as Mikaela Banes in the 2007 blockbuster *Transformers*, she's adored by movie fans everywhere. Famous for her dark hair and tattoos, she starred in *Jennifer's Body* in 2009, a film about a cheerleader possessed by demons. Yikes!

ZAC EFRON

Hollywood heartthrob, Zac (born 1987), is the star of hit movies such as *Charlie St. Cloud* and *17 Again*. He got his big break in 2006 when he was picked to play Troy Bolton in *High School Musical*. Zac says that he used to be scared of speaking in front of people. Not any more!

AND THE WINNER IS...

Movie stars love a big night out, especially if there's an award on offer. So we're rolling out the red carpet for some of the showbiz events of the year...

> **DID YOU KNOW?**
> The most Oscars ever won by a single film is 11. This has happened three times – Ben Hur (1959), Titanic (1997) and Lord of the Rings: Return of the King (2003).

The Oscars

The Oscars are the most famous film awards in the world. Begun in 1929, they're voted for by the members of the Academy of Motion Pictures in Hollywood. Winners receive a golden statue, called an Oscar (supposedly named after someone's uncle) and make a speech. The Oscars on the left are giant display versions.

http://www.oscars.org

WEBtag Official website of the Academy Awards®.

The Baftas

The Baftas (British Academy of Film and Television Awards) are held every year in London. There are awards for the best films, TV programmes, video games and animation. Winning a Bafta will give your career a serious boost and you also get a gold statue in the shape of a theatrical mask.

Palme d'Or

The Palme d'Or ('Golden Palm') is the prize given to the Best Feature Film at the Cannes Film Festival in France. It was first awarded in 1955. A palm, like the one held here by Penelope Cruz, is made of 24-carat gold and crystal, and is presented to the winner.

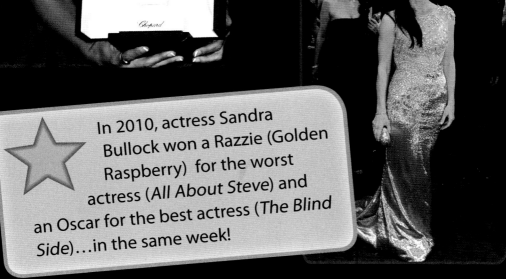

In 2010, actress Sandra Bullock won a Razzie (Golden Raspberry) for the worst actress (*All About Steve*) and an Oscar for the best actress (*The Blind Side*)…in the same week!

MOVIE SLEEPOVER GAMES

Have a happening Hollywood party with these brilliant movie-themed sleepover games. If you're feeling creative, you could make some mini Oscar statues to give to the winners.

o Movie truth or dare?

Ask each other cringeworthy truth or dare questions about movie stars, such as 'Do you fancy X?' If you pick dare, choose one of these **forfeits** to do…

- o Sing your favourite song very slowly.
- o Tell your funniest joke.
- o Do an impression of a movie star.
- o Give an **OTT** Oscar acceptance speech.

Another cool thing to do is to get your guests to dress up and act out a scene from your favourite movie. Film and edit the results, then hold a 'World Premiere' of your own movie.

WEBtag Party planning website – click on the 'Kids Games' link.

http://www.purpletrail.com/ partytrail/party_planning

Oscars talent show

Hold your own Oscars talent show. You can act out scenes from your favourite movies, make up dance routines or sing a song from a musical. But do everything as badly as possible – it'll be much funnier. Give an award to the 'best' worst performance in each category.

Movie charades

Act out the title of a movie without using words. Your friends have to guess the movie. Before you start, agree how to show things like 'first **syllable**' and 'number of words'.

Movie star who am I?

Think of a famous movie star. Your friends have to guess who it is. But they can only ask you questions you can answer with a 'YES' or a 'NO', such as 'Does he have dark hair?'

HOLLYWOOD HAUNTS

For some real movie glitz and glamour, Hollywood, or 'Tinseltown' as it is also known, is the place to be. It is the world famous centre of the US film industry. Just check out these famous Hollywood haunts.

KODAK THEATRE

The Kodak Theatre is on Hollywood Boulevard. Once a year, the theatre is dressed up with a golden curtain and a sweeping red carpet, and plays host to the Oscars ceremony. The rest of the year, you can watch live concerts, plays and TV shows.

UNIVERSAL STUDIOS

Take a tour of the studios and get a behind-the-scenes look at how some of your favourite movies were made. Have your photo taken with Shrek, then hop on the Jurassic Park-themed ride that drops you down a 25-metre waterfall.

HOLLYWOOD SIGN

You can't miss this spectacular sign high up in the hills. It spells out 'Hollywood' in 14-metre high white letters and it's a star in its own right. In the 2010 movie, *Percy Jackson and the Olympians*, the entrance to the 'underworld' is hidden behind the sign.

http://www.walkof fame.com

WEBtag Click the 'Walk of Fame' link to find out more about its star names.

 Doris Day appeared in 39 films during her career.

WALK OF FAME

This world-famous pavement runs along Hollywood Boulevard. It is studded with more than 2,000 bronze-rimmed stars, featuring the names of famous celebrities.

MOVIE STAR MAKEOVER

Ever wished you looked more like a movie star? Follow our top tips for transforming yourself into a super-glam celeb. It's all about sparkle, glitter and gloss.

Amazing eyes...

Go for make-up in colours that complement your outfit, such as the pink and purple eyeshadow on the left. Choose shimmery eyeshadow, glitter eyeshadow and coloured mascara – just maybe not all at the same time!

Luscious lips...

For a movie-star pout, use lipliner to outline your lips, then fill in the colour. Blot your lips on a tissue, then add another coat of lippy and finish off with a slick of clear gloss.

WEBtag Makeover tips and cheats from the beauty experts at Maybelline.

http://www.maybelline.co.uk/MAKE_UP_TIPS.aspx

Fabulous hair...

Tie your hair into a ponytail, and pin it high on your head in an **updo**. Leave some hair to fall naturally at your neckline. The updo shown on the left was created by a professional hair stylist.

Gorgeous nails...

File your nails, then smooth them off. Paint them shocking pink or silver. Add a touch of extra glamour with some gorgeous stick-on gems.

If you're hosting the sleepover, set aside part of your bedroom as a star's dressing room. Add a mirror, lights and a comfy chair and spoil your guests with some party pampering.

BOLLYWOOD BLOCKBUSTERS

Never mind Hollywood, here's…Bollywood. It's India's enormous film industry, based in Mumbai (the city used to be called Bombay) and it's famous for its blockbusting movies and impossibly glamorous movie stars.

○ Most Bollywood movies have a bit of everything – singing, dancing, romance, comedy and action. They're known as 'masala' films after the Indian spice mix.

○ About 14 million Indians watch Bollywood movies every day.

Kareena Kapoor (centre) stars in *Sometimes Happy, Sometimes Sad*.

○ Bollywood movies are usually around three hours long, and sometimes even four. Luckily, there's always an **interval**.

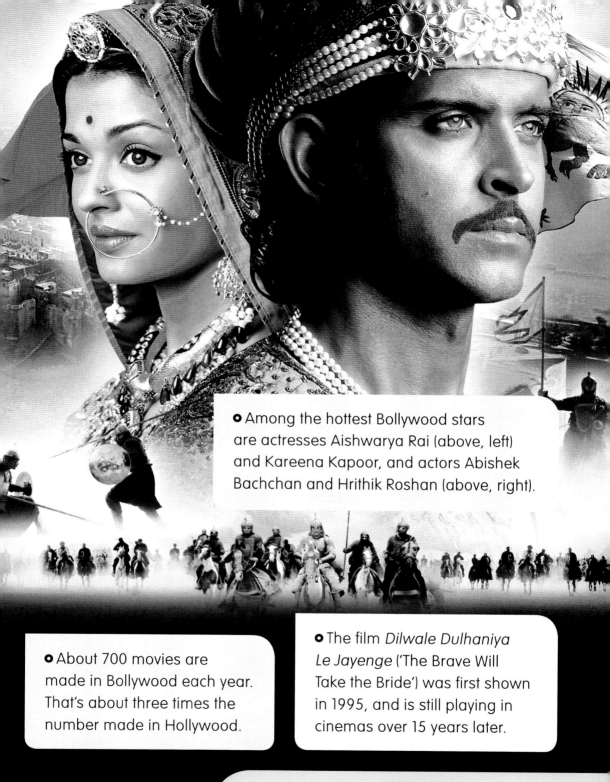

○ Among the hottest Bollywood stars are actresses Aishwarya Rai (above, left) and Kareena Kapoor, and actors Abishek Bachchan and Hrithik Roshan (above, right).

○ About 700 movies are made in Bollywood each year. That's about three times the number made in Hollywood.

○ The film *Dilwale Dulhaniya Le Jayenge* ('The Brave Will Take the Bride') was first shown in 1995, and is still playing in cinemas over 15 years later.

http://www.bollywoodworld.com

WEBtag Features up-to-date Bollywood news, plus trailers and photos.

MAKE ME A MOVIE STAR

Have you ever dreamed of becoming a movie star? Would you love to see your name up there in lights? Try this star-studded quiz to see if you've got what it takes...

1 You're off to the cinema. What films do you like watching best?
☆ **Anything – you could watch films all day.**
♥ **You only like musicals.**
❀ **You only like films if they're short.**

2 At your friend's karaoke party, you...
☆ **Hog the mic all party.**
♥ **Sing one song, then let someone else have a go.**
❀ **Pretend you've got a sore throat.**

3 Reading out a poem in front of the class is…
- ⭐ **Fantastic! You love the attention.**
- 🖤 **You'll do it, but you'd rather not.**
- ❀ **It's the most cringey thing you can think of.**

4 One thing you'd never miss is…
- ⭐ **Drama club**
- 🖤 **Gym club**
- ❀ **Your favourite TV soap.**

5 You've been invited to a party. What do you wear?
- ⭐ **Something glam and glitzy – you can't wear too many sequins.**
- 🖤 **Jeans and a smart T-shirt.**
- ❀ **You'd rather get your pjs on and get to bed.**

What your score means…

⭐ Mostly
You love being in the limelight and you'd make an ace leading actress. You have no problem putting on a performance and would fit right in with the red carpet crowd.

🖤 Mostly
You can take the celebrity life or leave it, though you'd rather someone else was the centre of attention instead of you. You might be better in a supporting role.

❀ Mostly
You're quite shy and the idea of people watching you makes you freak out big time. You'd be much better off behind the camera, rather than in front of it.

MOVIE STUNT DOUBLES

The movie world is not all glamour – there's hard work to be done too. Movie stunt-double girls are right in the action, riding motorbikes through fire or leaping from planes. Check out these experts...

HIDDEN TALENTS

Stunt men and women double up for movie stars in scenes that are risky or need special skills. Michiko Nishiwaki (right) doubles for Lucy Liu in many of her action scenes. The work of stunt doubles often goes unnoticed by movie audiences.

DID YOU KNOW?
In the *Twilight Saga: New Moon*, there's a scene where actress Ashley Greene drives a fast car down a country lane. But look closely. The driver's actually a stunt double and what's more, she's a man in a wig!

SPECIAL SKILLS

Stunt doubles come from many backgrounds, including martial arts and motor sports. Their skills, such as high-speed racing and leaping through windows, make smash-hit movies. Stunt doubles can go on to become stunt **co-ordinators**.

Jennifer Caputo (left), is a stunt double for musician and actress Sheryl Crow.

http://www.jennifer-caputo.com

WEBtag Jennifer's website features videos of her stunts.

PERFECT PARTY FOOD

When your guests get hungry, serve up delicious cupcakes, and seriously chic 'mocktails'. Here are some recipes...

Cute cupcakes

You'll need (makes 12):
100 g self-raising flour
100 g butter or margarine
100 g caster sugar
2 eggs
1/2 teaspoon vanilla essence

What to do:
1 Preheat the oven to 190° C.

2 Put the ingredients in a large bowl and beat until the mixture is glossy and smooth.

3 Put some paper cupcake cases into a cupcake tin, and fill them to just under halfway.

4 Put them in the oven and bake for 10-12 minutes, until they're golden-brown and springy to the touch.

5 Leave them to cool on a wire rack before decorating – see panel on right for suggestions.

Anita says: depending on your age, you may need to ask an adult for help.

To make icing, beat 75 g butter until it's soft, then add 175 g icing sugar and mix until smooth. Spread a little on each cupcake. Then decorate with Hollywood-style silver balls, stars and edible glitter. You could also add cocoa powder to the cupcake mixture and add chocolate to the icing for a super chocolate fix.

Dazzling drinks

Serve sparkling non-alcoholic mocktails in cocktail glasses. Try 'frosting' each glass first. Rub the rim with a slice of lemon, then carefully dip it into some sugar so it coats all of the rim. Or create super-star smoothies in tall milkshake glasses, then add Hollywood extras, such as kiwi fruit or strawberries.

LIGHTS, CAMERA, ACTION!

How do your favourite movies get to the big screen? It takes months of hard work and a budget running into millions of pounds. Here's a sneak peek behind-the-scenes at how a movie is made...

PRINCE OF PERSIA

Prince of Persia: The Sands of Time stars Jake Gyllenhaal and Gemma Arterton. They play Prince Dastan and Princess Tamina in a quest to save Persia from falling under the rule of evil Nizam (Ben Kingsley). The movie is directed by Mike Newell, who also directed Harry Potter and the Goblet of Fire in 2005.

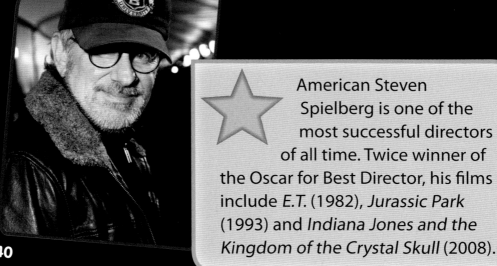

American Steven Spielberg is one of the most successful directors of all time. Twice winner of the Oscar for Best Director, his films include E.T. (1982), Jurassic Park (1993) and Indiana Jones and the Kingdom of the Crystal Skull (2008).

1. A screenwriter creates a working script, called a screenplay, that contains the actors' lines, as well as instructions for the shoot. Once the screenplay is finished, production starts. *Prince of Persia* had three screenwriters! The director has to turn the words into pictures on the screen. He or she has overall responsibility for the film.

2. The producer hires the crew. Hundreds of people are involved, including film editors, **cinematographers**, actors and **extras** (shown).

3. The casting director finds the best actors or actresses for the different roles. Then it's over to them to bring the characters in the movie to life.

4. The movie is shot partly in a studio, and partly on location. This means building sets, designing costumes and planning scenes from start to finish.

5. Filming begins and the actors shoot their scenes under the director's eagle eye. It may need several **takes** to get a scene right. Much of *Prince of Persia* was shot in Morocco.
6. The director gives specific instructions to achieve the right shot. Here Mike Newell is talking to Gemma Arterton.

7. The film is still far from finished. In the editing room, the editor turns metres of film into a watchable movie.

8. Music is added, and any special effects. At last, the final cut is ready – that's the version the audience sees. There may still be some last-minute tweaks if the director is not totally happy.

9. Finally, it's the night of the premiere. Fans turn out to greet the stars, shown here is Daud Shah (left) who plays Asoka. The film is now ready for release, and that's a wrap, as they say in the movies.

GLOSSARY

3-D ⊖ short for 'three dimensional'. Wearing special glasses makes the characters and scenery look incredibly life-like.

'A' list ⊖ the most famous and sought-after celebrities.

Audition ⊖ when an actor gives a short performance to show his or her suitability for a part in a movie.

Blockbusters ⊖ big-budget movies that turn out to be smash hits.

Celluloid ⊖ the type of film used to take movies.

Cinematographer ⊖ people who take pictures with a movie camera.

Co-ordinator ⊖ in the movies, stunt co-ordinators are people who make sure that stunts run smoothly and on time.

Extras ⊖ actors and actresses with very minor parts – often in the background, for example, as part of a street scene.

Forfeit ⊖ something that you have to do if you lose a game.

Interval ⊖ a short break between parts of a movie.

Nominees ⊖ a person chosen to be in the running for a prize or award.

On location ⊖ when filming is done in a location (place) outside a studio.

OTT ⊖ short for 'Over The Top', meaning going to extremes.

Plot ⊖ the stories or plan of movies.

Shot ⊖ in movie language, shot means when a particular scene is filmed.

Syllable ⊖ a sound that is part of a word.

Takes ⊖ the filming of scenes in a movie.

Talkie ⊖ the name given to an early film that has a soundtrack.

Updo ⊖ a type of hairstyle where the hair is piled up on top of the head.

VIP ⊖ short for 'Very Important Person'.

MORE WEBSITES

http://www.pixar.com
Home of Pixar Animation, creators of *Toy Story*, *WALL-E* and *Monsters Inc.* Features a 'how we move a movie' section and artist's corner.

http://www.screenonline.org.uk/film/index.html
Part of the British Film Institute (BFI) website, featuring an interactive timeline, genre information and British film history from the 1890s to 2000s.

http://www.www.kodaktheatre.com
Find out more about the Kodak Theatre, its history and the Academy Awards® which are held there.

http://www.festival-cannes.com
International portal of the Cannes Film Festival which includes the festival's history, festival posters and award news.

http://www.dreamworksanimation.com
Home of Dreamworks Animation, creators of *Shrek*, *Madagascar*, *How To Train Your Dragon* and *Kung Fu Panda*. Features trailers.

http://adisney.go.com/disneypictures/princeofpersia
Disney's *Prince of Persia* website, which features videos, photo galleries and downloadables. Plus there are sound snippets of music featured in the movie.

INDEX